TIME FOR KIDS®

DEVELOPING READER 2 · Science Scoops

Ants!

By the Editors of TIME FOR KIDS
WITH BRENDA IASEVOLI

HarperCollinsPublishers

About the Author: Brenda Iasevoli has worked as a fourth-grade teacher, a writer, and an editor. As a teacher, she enjoyed watching students grow and learn. As an editor at TFK, she relishes writing about topics that she might not have learned about otherwise.

To Judith Ann O'Neill, because ants aren't the only hard workers with tireless dedication to their families.

Special thanks to Corrie Saux of Harvard University and Alex Wild of myrmecos.net for their thoughtful answers to many questions.   *—B.I.*

Library of Congress Cataloging-in-Publication Data is available.

ISBN 0-06-057640-5 (pbk.) — ISBN 0-06-057641-3 (trade)

1 2 3 4 5 6 7 8 9 10
First Edition

Photography and Illustration Credits:
Cover: Charles Konig—© Proceeding of The National Academy of Sciences; cover insert: Mitsuhiko Imamori—Minden; cover flap: James H. Robinson—Photo Researchers; title page: Mitsuhiko Imamori—Minden; contents page: Fabio Colombini—Animals Animals; pp. 4–5: Alex Wild; pp. 6–7: Anne Reas; pp. 8–9: Alex Wild; pg. 8 (inset): Anne Reas; pp. 10–11: Alex Wild; pp. 12–13: Mark Moffett—Minden; pp. 14–15: Anthony Bannister—Gallo Images/Corbis; pp. 16–17: Jagdish Agarwal—SCPhotos/Alamy; pg. 16 (inset): Barry Runk/Stan/Grant Heilman; pp. 18–19: Premaphotos/Naturepl.com; pg. 18 (inset): Mark Moffett—Minden; pp. 20–21: Mark Moffett—Minden; pp. 22–23: Penny Tweedie—Corbis; pg. 23 (inset): Leo Meier—Australian Picture Library/Corbis; pp. 24–25: Look GMBH/Estock Photo; pp. 26–27: NaturePicks/Alamy; pp. 28–29: Alex Wild; pg. 28 (inset): Time Life Pictures/Getty Images; pp. 30–31: Charlotte Thege—Peter Arnold; pg. 31 (inset): Alex Wild; pg. 32 (anthill): Jagdish Agarwal—SCPhotos/Alamy; pg. 32 (cocoon): Anthony Bannister—Gallo Images/Corbis; pg. 32 (colony): Mark Moffett—Minden; pg. 32 (larva): Mark Moffett—Minden; pg. 32 (mandibles): Anthony Bannister—Gallo Images/Corbis; pg. 32 (queen): Alex Wild; pg. 32 (Fun Fact): John Courtney

Acknowledgments:
For TIME For Kids: Editorial Director: Keith Garton; Editor: Nelida Gonzalez Cutler; Art Director: Rachel Smith; Photography Editor: Jill Tatara

 **Check us out at www.timeforkids.com**

CONTENTS

Chapter 1: The Ants Go Marching **4**

Chapter 2: All in the Family **10**

Chapter 3: Snack Attack! **20**

Chapter 4: Ants and Enemies **26**

Did You Know? **31**

Words to Know **32**

Ant from
Brazil

CHAPTER ONE

The Ants Go

Citronella
ants

Marching

An army of ants is hard at work.
Ants are busy digging.
They are crawling on the ground.
They are searching for food.

Ants are insects.

Like all insects, they have six legs
and three body parts.
They have a hard covering, much like a shell.
Here are the parts of a queen ant.

Wings
Only queens and
male ants have wings.
These ants fly up
into the sky to mate.

Abdomen
The abdomen
holds the organs.
It is also where
ants store food.

Antennas
These feelers help ants to touch, taste, and smell. Ants also use their antennas to communicate with each other.

Thorax
The six legs are attached to the thorax.

Mandibles
Ants have strong jaws called mandibles. They are used to dig, cut, bite, and carry objects.

Eyes
Ants have compound eyes that help them sense motion.

Head
The head holds the brain, eyes, and antennas.

Legs
Ants have six legs that help them to run, climb, and dig.

How Big?

The atomic ant is the smallest ant. It is about the size of a grain of sand!

The giant tropical hunting ant is the biggest ant. It can grow to be more than one and one-half inches long!

Green head ants

There are nearly twelve thousand different kinds of ants.
They can be brown, green, black, red, yellow, purple, or blue.
Ants live everywhere except Antarctica.

CHAPTER TWO

All in the Family

A queen ant
and workers

Most ants live in groups called colonies.
A colony has three types of ants:
queens, males, and workers.
Queens have two important jobs.
They mate with male ants and lay eggs.

A fire ant queen
with other fire ants,
larvas, and pupas

**When an egg hatches,
a larva appears.**

The larva spins a silky cocoon around itself.
This ant is now called a pupa.
The pupa grows and grows inside the cocoon.

Spotted sugar worker
ants with cocoons

Worker ants bite open the cocoon.
The grown ant comes out!
Workers take care of the queen
and younger ants.
They also protect the colony.

A harvester
ant tunnel

Ant homes are called nests.

Most ants build their nests underground.
They dig tunnels and rooms.
They carry the extra dirt outside.
It forms an anthill.

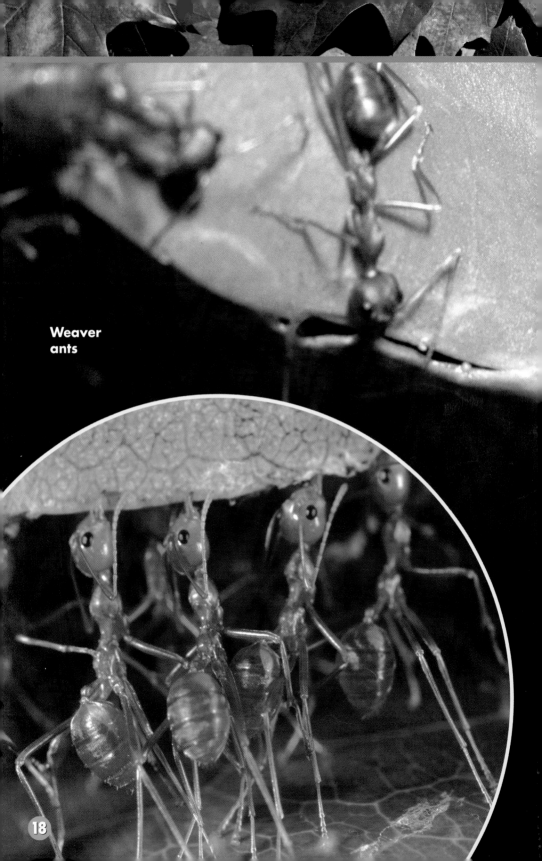

Weaver
ants

18

Weaver ants build their nests in trees.

Some ants hold the edges of leaves.
Other workers carry larvas
along the edges.
Larva silk glues the leaves together.

CHAPTER THREE

Snack Attack!

A harvester ant
with a seed

Ants eat both plants and animals.
They look for seeds, fruit, bread,
and even other insects.
Ants carry food back to the colony
to share.

Honey pot
ants

Some honey pot ants store a juice called honeydew.

When a honey pot ant is hungry, it taps its antennas on a fat ant. The fat honey pot ant spits honeydew into the mouth of the hungry ant.

Leaf cutter ants

Leaf cutter ants are farmers.
They cut and chew leaves with
their sharp mandibles.
Then they make a paste.
The paste is used to grow a garden.

Ants and

A bee killer bug
and a tiny ant

Enemies

Ants have many enemies. Spiders, birds, lizards, anteaters, and other animals eat ants. But ants will fight to protect themselves and their colony.

Spotlight

Charles Darwin was a famous English scientist.
He was born in 1809.
Darwin studied how plants and animals developed over time.
No living thing was too small to study, not even ants.
Darwin noticed that sometimes ants behaved just like humans!

Green tree ants fighting

Ants fight each other.
They use their mandibles to bite.
Some ants squirt poison from
their mouths into their enemies.

Ants from
Kenya

Ants have been on the earth for millions of years.

Giant dinosaurs disappeared.
But tiny ants survived.
Remember that the next time ants invade your picnic!

Did You Know?

Army ants cross rivers! They link their bodies together to build bridges.

Many queen ants can live for more than ten years.

Worker ants are all female.

The slaver ant steals cocoons from other ant colonies. The ant baby is forced to work when it grows up.

Ants can dig tunnels as deep as thirty-five feet.